Congratulations, You Passed! Test-taking Techniques & Tips for Passing Exams

A Left Brain And Right Brain Approach

Congratulations, You Passed!

Test-taking Techniques & Tips for Passing Exams

A Left Brain And Right Brain Approach

By Betty McKenzie Moore

Foreword by Christopher I. Moore

bmoore@TheEmploymentFront.com.

Published in the United States of America by The Employment Front, LLC, Fayetteville, GA

ISBN: 978-0-9908734-1-9 Paperback

Book Cover design by Daniel Burgos
Edited by John R. McHugh & Christopher I. Moore

This Book is dedicated:

To my husband, Calvin, for his love and unwavering support in everything I do.

TABLE OF CONTENTS

Foreword

I think it's safe to say that most people have at least one supposedly irrational fear, or phobia. Just taking a quick glance at an online list of phobias (from the aptly named phobialist.com) reveals hundreds of them! Some of my favorites include: ombrophobia (fear of rain), agoraphobia (fear of open spaces), triskaidekaphobia (fear of the number 13), coulrophobia (fear of clowns), and even xanthophobia (fear of the color yellow). Unfortunately, this book cannot help you with any of those. There is one, however with which I, myself, am intimately acquainted—testophobia, the fear of (you guessed it!) taking tests. The symptoms of this condition (increased heart rate, restlessness, loss of concentration, and low self-esteem just to name a few) stem from the anxiety one experiences before and/or during any testing situation. Given how much importance parents, schools, scholarship committees, and even potential employers can place on test scores, it's not hard to understand where that pressure comes from. And that is precisely where *Congratulations, You Passed! Test-taking Techniques & Tips for Passing Exams* comes in. The skills and tips presented in this book aim to take the fear of the unknown out of the test-taking equation. It all comes down to being prepared for not only *what* question is being asked but also *how* the question is being asked. Your course materials will help you with the former; this book will cover the latter.

My mom has been teaching Human Resources' PHR and SPHR certification test prep classes for longer than I can remember and, ever since I was little, has been using the same techniques you will find here on me as I prepared for all of my standardized testing throughout my primary academic career. Of course, back then, I was completely ignorant to the actual methodology of my study plan. I just did what I was told (well, *most* of the time). As I would later discover, she was developing a foundation for testing that is still just as relevant now (more than a decade later) as it was then. All tests have the same goal: for you to express to your understanding and mastery of a given subject. Furthermore, they all attempt to accomplish that in a similar matter. Whether you're in high school preparing for the SAT or ACT or a post-college graduate looking at business schools and getting ready for the GMAT or a business professional preparing for a major certification exam, these techniques are transferable. And if you have even the slightest amount of anxiety when it comes to taking these tests, you have come to the right place. I can assure you that once you have a game plan to outsmart the test makers, themselves, they won't seem nearly as scary! Oh, by the way, using these tips and techniques, I graduated from Georgia Tech with a B.S. Degree in Electrical Engineering.

GOOD LUCK!

Chris

Christopher I. Moore

About My Approach

I wrote this book with the same approach I use to teach classes or conduct the preparatory course for the Human Resources' PHR (Professional in Human Resources) and SPHR (Senior Professional in Human Resources) certification exams. Namely, my test-taking techniques and tips will incite you to utilize both your Left Brain and Right Brain in preparing to pass your exam. If you are like most people, using your Left Brain will be easier for you because it is the conscious part of the brain that controls such things as:

Language,

Number skills,

Analytical skills,

Logic,

Mathematics,

Facts,

Critical thinking, etc.

The **Left Brain is the Verbal** part of our thinking. Being the conscious part of our minds, we tend to be very skilled at using it.

Unfortunately, most people do not develop their Right Brain nor consciously use it to their advantage. The Right Brain sometimes called the subconscious or unconscious part of our mind is very powerful. When we look into studies about our Right Brain, we discover its magnificent, creative powers. The Right Brain can among other things:

Create visual memory and creative thinking,

Store nonverbal memory of objects,

Make complex mental associations,

Understand a large number of words,

Call up a mental image and make everything in your visual span of that image available to you at once,

Produce more results than just memorizing because it is based on thinking,

Hold an enormous amount of information, etc.

The **Right Brain is the Visual** part of our thinking.

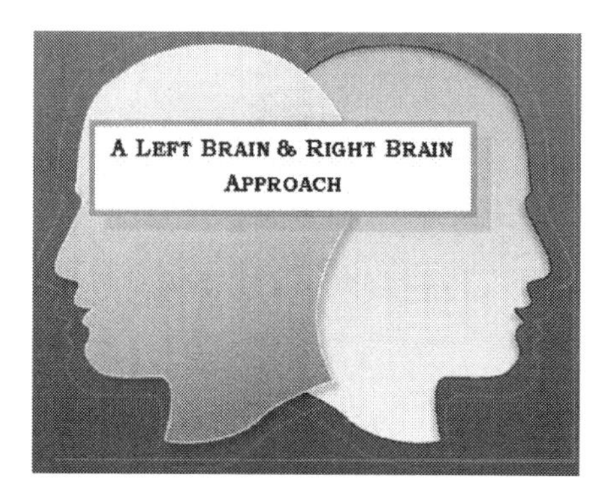

The truth is when you partner your visual thinking with your verbal thinking (subconscious and conscious), they can work together in completing tasks, solving problems, and passing exams.

According to the late Graham Wallas in his book ***Art of Thought***, the creative process has four stages:

Graham Wallas
31st May 1858 - 9th August 1932

English Social Psychologist

Art of Thought - The Model of Creativity
Published in 1926.

"Stage One – **Preparation Stage** which consists of gathering relevant information and narrowing the problem down until the obstacles are visible. *(Left Brain Activity)*

Stage Two – **Incubation Stage** the period in which the unconscious part of the brain works on the problem. (*Right Brain Activity)*

Stage Three – **Illumination Stage** where intuition and insight produce possible solutions to the problem. (*Right Brain Activity)*

Stage Four – **Verification Stage** in which intuitive solutions are logically tested for validity then organized and elaborated into a finished solution." (*Left Brian Activity)*

Although his book is no longer in publication, many psychologists still support his findings. Using Graham Wallas' four stages, creative problem solving is when you make a discovery nonverbally and then verbalize your feelings.

My experience is that when a student learns a concept in this creative problem solving way there is less need to memorize it because s/he will know it in a deeper more intuitive manner. The student learns the concept in both a verbal and nonverbal sense. A single word or stem can act as a stimulus for the Right Brain to make an association to an image that leads the student to an answer to a problem. The testing-taking techniques and tips in this book reflect this creative problem solving approach.

As you start your journey to passing your exam, I will be there with you through this book. Giving you the benefits of my 15 years of experience in helping others pass their exams, I will encourage you to use both your Left Brain and Right Brain so you can pass your exam too.

I want to thank you for allowing me to be a part of your learning and look forward to you Passing your exam. Now, let's get started...

As we start the journey to Your Exam day, please follow the tips and test-taking techniques in the order presented.

Tip 1: First Things First

There are five important actions I suggest you complete before you do anything else. They are your First Things First actions:

1. First, you need to **define your "Why?"** Why do you want to pass this test/exam? What will it mean to you? Your "Why" must be compelling, bigger than you, and clearly stated. Do you want to pass this test/exam so you can get a better job? Or do you want to increase your financial security? Or maybe you want to attend your favorite college? Once you define your "Why", write it down on a piece of paper or index card and review it every day. The main reason this action is so important is because you will be spending a lot of time preparing

for your exam. A strong, well-written "Why," will help keep you focused, encouraged and determined to continue no matter how tough it becomes. **Your Why is *Your Motivation.***

2. Secondly, you need to **create a "Vision" of passing the exam**. You create this vision by visualizing. According to Webster, to visualize is "to form a mental image of something not present to the sight." When you visualize, you create a vision or force of creative power. In creating this mental image of passing the exam, include vivid details in your image. Spell out such things as what you are wearing, who you call first to share the great news, that person's reaction to your great news, what you will do to celebrate, etc. Prepare a mental image of

the words...Congratulations, You Passed. **Your Vision is *Your Dream*.**

3. Next, **decide on your 'Exam Date."** Make sure your date is not during a real busy time for you at work or home. Keep in mind, though, that you will always be busy and that your "Why" is important enough for you to invest time in yourself – something no one else can do for you. Once you know the date, determine how many weeks there are before that date and how many hours each week you need to spend studying. **Your Exam Date is Your Destination.**

4. Then, **meet with your Family and/or Friends**. During this meeting, share your "Why" and explain to them that you need their support during the next

number of weeks or months. This conversation is critical because it gives those close to you an understanding up front of what you will be doing during your spare time. It can also get your family and/or friends involved in your journey because they can help ensure you have quiet time when you study; and help hold you accountable to your "Why" if you get off course and stop studying when you should. **Your Family and Friends Are Your Support.**

5. Finally, make a commitment and **Register for the exam**. Since most major exams have a fee, paying the money for the exam will increase your commitment. **Your Registration is Your Commitment.**

In Review, please remember to complete the First

things First actions…

Your Why – Your Motivation

Your Vision – Your Dream

Your Exam Date – Your Destination

Your Family/Friends – Your Support

Your Registration – Your Commitment

PLAN
DO
STUDY
ACT

Tip 2: Developing Your Study Plan

Your study plan is your map for your journey to Exam Day. With that in mind, your plan must be solid and complete that includes realistic, attainable, and detailed actions. This book outlines the majority of the critical actions for your plan. But, you must decide how and when you will complete then. In addition, you need to make a decision on how much "Time" you can realistically devote to studying. Here are some tips to complete your Plan:

1. Time - you must devote time to your exam preparation. Treat this time like it is a part-time job. The beauty of this part-time job is that you know it

will end on Exam Day. I recommend you spend at least 10-20 hours per week studying. Use your study time either reading the materials or taking practice exams.

2. Gather your materials:

The reading materials on the body of knowledge for the exam,

Tape recorder or recording device *–optional*,

A dictionary,

A spiral notebook or digital document for taking your notes,

Practice exams,

A copy of your "Why,"

Your "Visual Image" of passing the exam.

3. Follow the steps outlined in Tips 3 through 12 in the order presented in this book.

4. Set a completion date for you to finish reading the materials.

5. Learn the "Test-taking Techniques" by heart.

6. Devote 80% of your study time to practicing taking exams using the "Test-taking Techniques."

7. Decide if you will join a study group or preparatory course. Joining a study group has many positive consequences. Such as, the group provides reinforcement of your learning, affiliation with other students with the same goal, accountability to your study plan. Be aware, that most study groups or prep courses cost money. If you cannot afford a

group or course, I recommend you pretend you are in a group by giving a family member or friend weekly updates on your progress.

8. Get a study partner. Just like the study group, a study partner can help you stay focused and determined to follow through on your study plan.

9. Everyday…

Read your "Why"
Visualize passing the "Exam"…visualize the words *Congratulations, You Passed!*

Tip 3: Taking Notes

As you read the materials, it is important to take notes of key concepts, facts and important information. I recommend that you take notes in a spiral notebook so that you can keep all of your study materials in one place. Another option is that you may take your notes digitally using a word processing application such as Microsoft Word. Since your reading and study time will last several weeks, it is critical that you organize your notes for easy retrieval in your final days of study before the exam. In order to do that effectively, you should prepare your notebook or digital document prior to reading your materials; and once you start reading, record your notes in a meaningful way. The following steps will assist you; I included steps for both options. The example for taking your notes digitally is in Microsoft Word.

Using a Spiral Notebook

1. Obtain an unused spiral notebook. If you have a lot of materials to read, you may need more than one notebook. If you end up with more than one notebook, make sure you number them in chronological order.

2. In the front of the notebook save the first five pages for completing a Table of Contents for a description of information in the notebook. Since you are just starting your reading, you do not know how many pages of notes you will take. You probably will not need five pages for your Table of Contents. I suggest reserving five to ensure you

have enough. These five pages will not be a part of your pages for taking notes.

3. For the remaining pages in your notebook or pages six through the last page in the notebook, number the pages starting with the number one on page six. You may place the page number at the top or bottom of the page. I typically place my page numbers in the top right-hand corner of the pages.

4. Your notebook is now ready for you to take your notes as you read. Keep in mind, you should only record in your notebook key concepts, important information and not everything you read.

5. When you take notes, record your information on your numbered note pages. After you finish

entering your notes on a key piece of information, go to the Table of Contents and record that entry with the name of the concept or important information and the starting page of that information as the page number for the Table of Contents item.

It looks something like this: Sample Notes – Using a Spiral Notebook

TABLE OF CONTENTS

SWOT Analysis (1)

S *= Strengths within the organization. Examples include employees' tenure, quality products and services, etc.*

***W** = Weakness within the organization. Examples include outdated equipment, untrained employees, etc.*

***O** = Opportunity outside the organization. Examples include changes in laws, advances in technology, etc.*

***T** = Threats outside the organization. Examples include a new competitor moving into the marketplace, etc.*

Maslow's Theory (3)

Maslow's theory states that humans have five basic needs. He called them Hierarchy of Needs. They are:

1. Physical Needs – food, water, shelter

2. Safety and Security – freedom from war, or other threats, etc.

3. Belonging and Love – family, friends, etc.

4. Esteem – approval of family, friends, etc.

5. Self-Actualization – education, religion, personal growth

Using Microsoft Word

1. When using Microsoft Word for taking your notes, create your document and save it in a special folder on your device. It looks like this:

Start with a blank document
1. Click the **file Button**, and then click **New**.
2. Click **Blank document**, and then click **Create**.
3. Make the changes that you want to the margin settings, page size and orientation, styles, and other formats.
4. Click the **file Button**, and then click **Save As**.
5. In the **Save As** dialog give the new document a file name,
6. Then click **Save**.

2. For creating a Table of Contents in Word, go to the "Reference" tab and click insert a Table of Contents or TOC. The help function in Word will give you step by step instructions. The "Reference" tab looks like this:

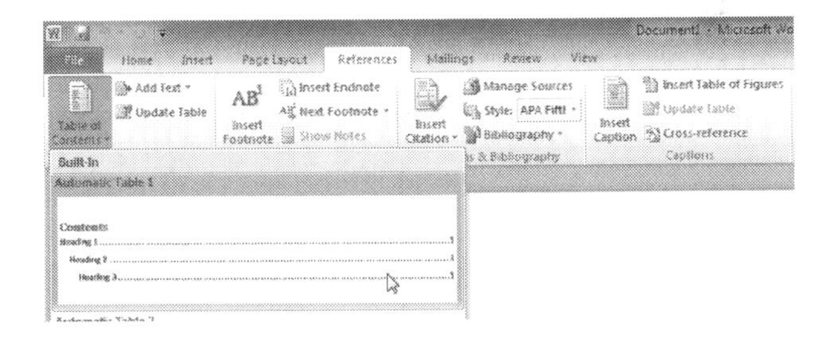

3. When using Word, include the page numbering function to number your pages; it is under the "Insert" tab.

4. In Word, just refresh your entire Table of Contents by placing your cursor anywhere within your Table of Contents and clicking update Table or

you can update your table under the "Reference" tab.

It looks something like this: Sample Notes – Using Microsoft Word

Table of Contents

Page | 19

Protein Sources

There are many great sources of protein and vital nutrient that help build muscle. Sources include these foods:

Meats such as beef, lamb, pork, chicken,

Eggs,

Beans and Peas such as black beans, black-eyed peas, legumes like chickpeas, soy beans,

Tofu a processed soy bean product,

Seafood,

Nuts.

Page | 19

Spoken Languages

The following are some of the languages spoken in different parts of the world:

Languages	Country
Chinese	China
Portuguese	Portugal
Javanese	Indonesia
Hindi, Telugu, Tamil	India
Spanish	Spain
Bengali	Bangladesh, some people in India
English	United States
Swahili	Kenya

Page | 20

Budgeting Models

In accounting, businesses use budgeting models to plan for company expenses. Examples are:

Incremental budgeting – a budgeting model that takes a previous year's budget and adds an incremental increase such as 4% to the new budget period.

Zero-based budgeting – a budgeting model that requires starting a new budget from zero or scratch with each proposed expense being justified before it is included in the budget.

By organizing and taking your notes in this manner, you accomplish two things. That is, you will be able to retrieve key concepts and information quickly when you go back to them during your study time; and you will help your Right Brain record images of your notes.

In review, prepare your notebook or Word document for taking notes before you start reading.

Make sure you:

1. Number your pages,

2. Create a Table of Contents,

3. Record only key concepts or important information and not everything you read.

Now you are almost ready to start reading. Before you start reading, let's review the next tip – Tip 4: Your Dictionary.

REMEMBER

Prepare your note taking document before you start reading.

Record only key concepts, important information or facts and not everything you read.

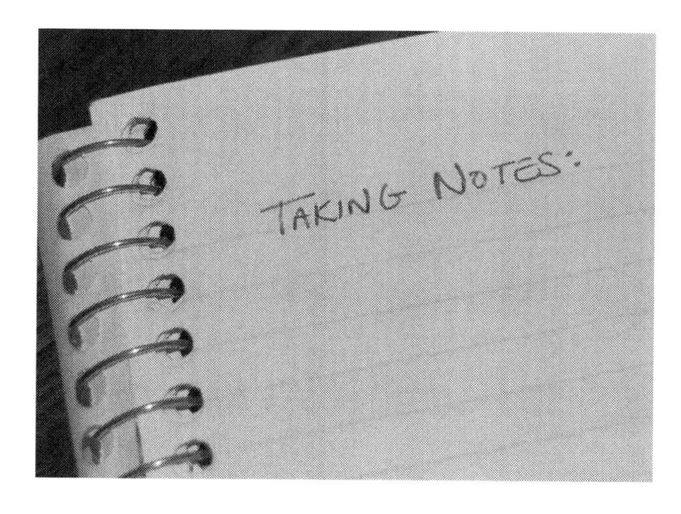

Tip 4: Your Dictionary

You are almost ready to start reading. The last item you need is a good dictionary. Your dictionary is your reading companion. While you are reading the materials, it is critical to understand the meaning of words that you may not be familiar with. The English language often has multiple meanings for a word. For example the word impact has five different meanings. Sometimes in exams the stem of the question may include the meaning that is not commonly used. In the case of the word impact depending on how it's used in a sentence, it could mean "results" or "effect." As you read and come across an unfamiliar word, look the word up in your dictionary and read all of the definitions. I use **Webster's New World College Dictionary, 4th Edition**. You can get the hard-copy or on-line version. Keep in mind, you may use any good dictionary not just the one I use. **Your Dictionary is *Your Reading Companion***.

Tip 5: Reading Your Materials

You prepared your notebook or digital document for taking notes and obtained a good dictionary now it's time to start reading. It is essential to "Read" your materials. Your reading materials cover the body of knowledge for your Exam. Since the exam questions come from this body of knowledge, there is great "Power" in reading it. Read everything including any glossary of terms. My recommendation is to read the materials once. Not trying to memorize, read it similar to reading a novel. If you are like many of my previous students, reading the materials once is a difficult concept to embrace. In that case, I suggest recording yourself as you read. By recording yourself while reading, you only have to read it once; and you are then able to listen to your recording anytime and anywhere to reinforce your learning.

As you read, take notes of key concepts, facts, and important information in your notebook or electronic document for review during study time later. Also, use your dictionary to make certain you understand everything you are reading. When you have a large amount of materials, you should read it in segments or modules, test your understanding of those materials, then read some more, test yourself and continue this pattern until you've read everything. (I'll talk about how to test your knowledge in the next chapter, Test-Taking Techniques.) By breaking up your reading, it will not be so taxing getting through the materials. In addition, it will help you solidify your understanding of the materials. Please remember, though, you should not complete a practice exam or test until you've read the materials covered in that exam or test. So, Read, Read, Read – reading gives you knowledge. The great power in reading is that it deposits information in the both the Left Brain and Right Brain. Remember your conscious and subconscious parts of your brain will work together to give you answers to questions. **Your Reading is *Your Power*.**

Did you know President John F. Kennedy could read 1200 words a minute?

I wish I could do that. What about you?

According to John F. Kennedy Presidential Library and Museum's Fast Facts about President John F. Kennedy on Reading it states:

"Reading Speed: John F. Kennedy could read 1200 words a minute. In 1954-1955 he attended meetings at the Foundation for Better Reading in Baltimore."

Test-Taking Techniques

1. **Read** the question thoroughly. **Select the "Stem" of the question**. In other words, determine what the question is really asking you. The Stem is a key word or phrase that explains the theme or main purpose of the question. It gives the plot of the question. The Stem connects the question to the right answer. It connects the subconscious part of the brain to the pre-recorded information about the question and brings that information to your consciousness to assist you in selecting the Best or most suitable answer to the question.

2. **Think about the possible answer**. Before looking at the choices, think about the possible answer.

3. **Read the Choices.** As you read the choices, decide for each choice if you will keep it as the possible answer or strike/disregard it because you know that choice is wrong.

4. **Re-read the Question**. From the choices you kept, re-read the question and the remaining choices. Make sure you re-read the question and supply each kept choice to the question separately. *Please note typically you will end up with two possible choices.*

5. **Select the Best choice as the answer to the question**.

6. **Think Positively.** Do not second guess your selected answer. Remember the subconscious part of your brain recognizes the stem and is now bringing that information to your consciousness.

7. **Answer all of the questions**. Make sure your answer every question. If there is a question(s) with content unfamiliar to you, make an informed guess by following the first five (5) techniques and selecting the choice that appears the most logical or reasonable. You have a fifty percent chance of answering the question correctly. When you leave a question(s) unanswered, you have a ZERO chance of getting it right because on most exams an

unanswered question is automatically a wrong answer.

8. **Review your selections** to ensure you answered everything the way you intended.

9. **Claim your reward in your mind**. Before submitting the exam for grading, visualize passing the exam. Prepare a mental image of the words…**Congratulations, You Passed.**

Tip 6: When You See These Words

When you see the following words in the stem of a question, it is very important that you understand what they mean relative to the answer. These words are easy to identify in the stem because they are often in all capital letters. They include:

1) BEST – when you see the word BEST, the question is asking you to select the most significant choice. All of the choices are important or good, but you are looking for the top choice, the one that has the most or highest weight. The most desirable, favorable or profitable choice…

2) MOST – when you see the word MOST, the question is asking you for the choice that has the highest degree of significance. The greatest in amount, quantity, degree or extent choice...

3) LEAST – when you see the word LEAST, the question is asking you for the choice that has the smallest importance. The slightest in size, degree or importance choice...

4) FIRST – when you see the word FIRST, the question is asking you for the choice that is the number one step. The foremost in rank, quality, importance or principal choice...

5) PRIMARY – when you see the word PRIMARY, the question is asking you for the choice that is the main reason or first reason. The chief, principal or fundamental choice...

6) NOT – when you see the word NOT, the question is asking you for the choice that has no connection to the question. The unrelated or irrelevant choice...

7) EXCEPT – when you see the word EXCEPT, the question is asking you for the only choice that is not related to the question. The leave out or omit choice...

Remember, when you see these words in the stem of a question be mindful of what they mean.

BEST

MOST

LEAST

FIRST

PRIMARY

NOT

EXCEPT

Tip 7: Practice Exams

Taking practice exams will increase your skills in using the Test-Taking Techniques and understanding the body of knowledge from your reading. Having secured practice exams, it's time for you to start using them as part of your study. One of the Major Keys to Passing Your Exam is being skilled at taking exams. You gain this skill by taking practice exams using the Test-Taking Techniques. Once you complete your reading, you should spend the majority of your study time taking practice exams over and over until you have scores of 90% or higher on each exam you take.

Here is how it works:

1. First read the materials that the exam covers.

2. Using the practice exam questions, apply the first six Test-Taking Techniques to find the answers. *(Please note, you will use Test-Taking Techniques seven – nine only on Exam Day.)*

Please review the following Sample Practice Exam that demonstrates how to apply the Test-Taking Techniques when answering questions. The reading materials for the 5 questions in this Sample Practice Exam are in the text right above each practice question. As you complete this exam, you may find the process repetitious. It is this way by design because I am showing you the proper way to apply the Test-Taking Techniques to questions. It is very important that you work through this demo and concentrate on memorizing each Test-Taking Technique.

Sample Practice Exam

Reading Material on Nutrition

There are many great sources of protein and vital nutrient that help build muscle. Sources include these foods:

Meats such as beef, lamb, pork, chicken,

Eggs,

Beans and Peas such as black beans, black-eyed peas, legumes like chickpeas, soy beans,

Tofu a processed soy bean product,

Seafood,

Nuts.

Question on nutrition:

1. Read the question thoroughly. Select the "Stem" of the question. In other words, determine what the question is really asking you. The Stem is a key word or phrase that explains the theme or main purpose of the question. It gives the plot of the question. The Stem connects the question to the right answer. It connects the subconscious part of the brain to the pre-recorded information about the question and brings that information to your

consciousness to assist you in selecting the Best or most suitable answer to the question.

Question: All of the following are great sources of protein EXCEPT?

The stem in this question is great sources of protein EXCEPT.

2. Think about the possible answer. Before looking at the choices, think about the possible answer.

I think the question is asking me to pick out something that is not a protein.

3. Read the Choices. As you read the choices, decide for each choice if you will keep it as the possible answer or strike/disregard it because you know that choice is wrong.

All of the following are great sources of protein EXCEPT?

a. Tofu
(I will ***strike this choice*** *because I know tofu is from soybean a protein source.)*

b. Apple
(I will ***keep this choice*** *because apple is a fruit.)*

c. Chickpeas

(I will ***keep this choice*** *because I am not clear on what it is.)*

d. Lamb
(I will ***strike this choice*** *because I know lamb is meat and meat is a protein source.)*

4. Re-read the Question. From the choices you kept, re-read the question and the remaining choices. Make sure you re-read the question and supply each kept choice to the question separately. *Please note typically you will end up with two possible choices.*

All of the following are great sources of protein EXCEPT? (b) Apple

All of the following are great sources of protein EXCEPT? (c) Chickpeas

5. Select the Best choice as the answer to the question.

I choose (b) Apple because I know apple is a fruit and the other choice sounds like a legume which is a protein.

6. Think Positively**.** Do not second guess your selected answer. Remember the subconscious part of your brain recognizes the stem and is now bringing that information to your consciousness.

Correct. Chickpeas are legumes. So (b) Apple is correct because it is a fruit.

Reading Material on SWOT:

S = Strengths within the organization. Examples include employees' tenure, quality products and services, etc.

W = Weakness within the organization. Examples include outdated equipment, untrained employees, etc.

O = Opportunity outside the organization. Examples include changes in laws, advances in technology, etc.

T = Threats outside the organization. Examples include a new competitor moving into the marketplace, etc.

Question on SWOT:

1. Read the question thoroughly. Select the "Stem" of the question. In other words, determine what the question is really asking you. The Stem is a key word or phrase that explains the theme or main purpose of the question. It gives the plot of the question. The Stem connects the question to the right answer. It connects the subconscious part of the brain to the pre-recorded information about the question and brings that information to your consciousness to assist you in selecting the Best or most suitable answer to the question.

Question: A small family owned business is developing a strategic plan for growing their business next year. Which of the following is an important analysis for understanding the company's internal strengths?

The stem in this question is the company's internal strengths.

2. Think about the possible answer. Before looking at the choices, think about the possible answer.

I think the question is asking me to pick out something inside the company that is good or positive.

3. Read the Choices. As you read the choices, decide for each choice if you will keep it as the possible answer or strike/disregard it because you know that choice is wrong.

A small family owned business is developing a strategic plan for growing their business next year. Which of the following is an important analysis for understanding the company's internal strengths?

a. Outdated equipment
*(I will **strike this choice** because outdated equipment is bad.)*

b. A federal requirement for clients

(I will ***keep this choice*** *because it could be positive.)*

c. Lack of training for new hires
(I will ***strike this choice*** *because it is negative.)*

d. Great customer service staff
(I will ***keep this choice*** *because it is positive.)*

4. Re-read the Question. From the choices you kept, re-read the question and the remaining choices. Make sure you re-read the question and supply each kept choice to the question separately. *Please note typically you will end up with two possible choices.*

A small family owned business is developing a strategic plan for growing their business next year. Which of the following is an important analysis for understanding the company's internal strengths? *(b) A federal requirement for clients*

A small family owned business is developing a strategic plan for growing their business next year. Which of the following is an important analysis for understanding the company's internal strengths? *(d) Great customer service staff*

5. Select the Best choice as the answer to the question.

I choose (d) Great customer service staff because that is a very positive internal attribute of the company.

6. Think Positively. Do not second guess your selected answer. Remember the subconscious part of your brain recognizes the stem and is now bringing that information to your consciousness.

Correct. A federal requirement is an outside influence on the company not an internal one. So the correct answer is (d) Great customer service staff an internal strength.

Reading Material on Spoken Languages:

The following are some of the languages spoken in different parts of the world:

Languages	Country
Chinese	China
Portuguese	Portugal
Javanese	Indonesia
Hindi, Telugu, Tamil	India
Spanish	Spain
Bengali	Bangladesh, some people in India
English	United States
Swahili	Kenya

Question on Language:

1. Read the question thoroughly. Select the "Stem" of the question. In other words, determine what the question is really asking you. The Stem is a key word or phrase that explains the theme or main purpose of the question. It gives the plot of the question. The Stem connects the question to the right answer. It connects the subconscious part of the brain to the pre-recorded information about the question and brings that information to your consciousness to assist you in selecting the Best or most suitable answer to the question.

Question: Jane has to travel to India for a business trip. She is concerned about understanding the spoken language of the people in India. Which of the following languages is she likely to encounter on her trip?

The stem of this question is languages likely to encounter.

2. Think about the possible answer. Before looking at the choices, think about the possible answer.

I think the question is asking me to pick out languages spoken in India.

3. Read the Choices. As you read the choices, decide for each choice if you will keep it as the possible answer or strike/disregard it because you know that choice is wrong.

Jane has to travel to India for a business trip. She is concerned about understanding the spoken language of the people in India. Which of the following languages is she likely to encounter on her trip?

a. Javanese and Spanish
*(**I will strike this choice** because Spanish is a language of Spain.)*

b. Swahili and English
*(**I will strike this choice** because Swahili is the language of Kenya.)*

c. Telugu and Hindi
*(**I will keep this choice** because Hindi is a language of India.)*

d. Bengali and Portuguese
*(**I will keep this choice** because Bengali is spoken in India.)*

4. Re-read the Question. From the choices you kept, re-read the question and the remaining choices. Make sure you re-read the question and supply each kept choice to the question separately. *Please note typically you will end up with two possible choices.*

Jane has to travel to India for a business trip. She is concerned about understanding the spoken language of the people in India. Which of the following languages is she likely to encounter on her trip? *(c) Telugu and Hindi*

Jane has to travel to India for a business trip. She is concerned about understanding the spoken language of the people in India. Which of the following languages is she likely to encounter on her trip? *(d) Bengali and Portuguese*

5. Select the Best choice as the answer to the question.

I choose (c) Telugu and Hindi because I know Hindi is a national language in India.

6. Think Positively. Do not second guess your selected answer. Remember the subconscious part of your brain recognizes the stem and is now bringing that information to your consciousness.

Correct. Even though many people in India speak Bengali, Portuguese is the language of Portugal. So the correct answer is (c) Telugu and Hindi.

Reading Material on Maslow's Theory:

Maslow's theory states that humans have five basic needs. He called them Hierarchy of Needs. They are:

1) Physical Needs—food, water, shelter

2) Safety and Security—freedom from war, or other threats, etc.

3) Belonging and Love—family, friends, etc.

4) Esteem—approval of family, friends, etc.

5) Self-Actualization—education, religion, personal growth

Question on Maslow:

1. Read the question thoroughly. Select the "Stem" of the question. In other words, determine what the question is really asking you. The Stem is a key word or phrase that explains the theme or main purpose of the question. It gives the plot of the question. The Stem connects the question to the right answer. It connects the subconscious part of the brain to the pre-recorded information about the question and brings that information to your consciousness to assist you in selecting the Best or most suitable answer to the question.

Question: Maslow's hierarchy of needs states human needs have a hierarchy of importance. Which of the following needs is the third need?

The stem of this question is the third need.

2. Think about the possible answer. Before looking at the choices, think about the possible answer.

I think the question is asking me about the hierarchy related to belonging.

3. Read the Choices. As you read the choices, decide for each choice if you will keep it as the possible answer or strike/disregard it because you know that choice is wrong.

Maslow's hierarchy of needs states human needs have a hierarchy of importance. Which of the following needs is the third need?

a. Food
*(I **will strike this choice** because it is a human's first need-Physical.)*

b. No war
*(I **will strike this choice** because it is a human's second need-Safety.)*

c. Love
*(I **will keep this choice** because it is a human's third need-Belonging.)*

d. Education
*(I **will strike this choice** because it is a human's fifth need-Self-Actualization.)*

4. Re-read the Question. From the choices you kept, re-read the question and the remaining choices. Make sure you re-read the question and supply each kept choice to the question separately. *Please note typically you will end up with two possible choices.*

Maslow's hierarchy of needs states human needs have a hierarchy of importance. Which of the following needs is the third need? *(c) Love*

5. Select the Best choice as the answer to the question.

I choose (c) Love because I know love is about feeling like you belong.

6. Think Positively. Do not second guess your selected answer. Remember the subconscious part of your brain recognizes the stem and is now bringing that information to your consciousness.

Correct. Love is a human need under the hierarchy of Belonging. In this example, I kept only one choice because I knew the others were wrong.

Reading Materials on Accounting Budgeting Models:

In accounting, businesses use budgeting models to plan for company expenses. Examples are:

Incremental budgeting – a budgeting model that takes a previous year's budget and adds an incremental increase such as 4% to the new budget period.

Zero-based budgeting – a budgeting model that requires starting a new budget from zero or scratch with each proposed expense being justified before it is included in the budget.

Question on types of Accounting Budgeting Models:

1. Read the question thoroughly. Select the "Stem" of the question. In other words, determine what the question is really asking you. The Stem is a key word or phrase that explains the theme or main purpose of the question. It gives the plot of the question. The Stem connects the question to the right answer. It connects the subconscious part of the brain to the pre-recorded information about the question and brings that information to your

consciousness to assist you in selecting the Best or most suitable answer to the question.

Question: John's company is expanding into a new market next year. His boss gave him a special project to recruit and train 10 new customer service representatives. This special project is key to growing the business. It's budgeting time. John's company uses the zero-based budgeting model. What should John do?

The stem in this question is zero-based budgeting.

2. Think about the possible answer. Before looking at the choices, think about the possible answer.

I think the question is asking me about starting from scratch for every item in the budget and providing the cost and justification for each.

3. Read the Choices. As you read the choices, decide for each choice if you will keep it as the possible answer or strike/disregard it because you know that choice is wrong.

John's company is expanding into a new market next year. His boss gave him a special project to recruit and train 10 new customer service representatives. It's budgeting time. John's company uses the zero-based budgeting model. What should John do?

a. Prepare his department's budget and include this special project's cost; and provide the cost and justification for that project and all other expense items in his budget
*(I **will keep this choice** because it has the word justification in it.)*

b. Exclude the special project from his budget because it came from his boss
*(I **will strike this choice** because the project must be paid for.)*

c. Ask his boss how she wants him to handle the expense for the special project
*(I **will keep this choice** because the boss may have special plans.)*

d. Add an incremental increase of 4% to the budget he submitted last year for the cost of this project
*(I **will strike this choice** because it describes the incremental budgeting model.)*

4. Re-read the Question. From the choices you kept, re-read the question and the remaining choices. Make sure you re-read the question and supply each kept choice to the question separately. *Please note typically you will end up with two possible choices.*

John's company is expanding into a new market next year. His boss gave him a special project to recruit and train 10 new customer service representatives. It's budgeting time. John's company uses the zero-based budgeting model. What should John do? *(a) Prepare his department's budget and include this special project's cost; and provide the cost and justification for that project and all other expense items in his budget*

John's company is expanding into a new market next year. His boss gave him a special project to recruit and train 10 new customer service representatives. It's budgeting time. John's company uses the zero-based budgeting model. What should John do? *(c) Ask his boss how she wants him to handle the expense for the special project*

5. Select the Best choice as the answer to the question.

I choose (a) Prepare his department's budget and include this special project's cost; and provide the cost and justification for that project and all other expense items in his budge. I selected this choice because it describes the zero-based budgeting model.

6. Think Positively**.** Do not second guess your selected answer. Remember the subconscious part of your brain recognizes the stem and is now bringing that information to your consciousness.

Correct. Zero-based budgeting requires justification for each budget expense.

Now that you have a demonstration of how to apply the Test-Taking Techniques, it's your turn to practice applying them.

So, Practice…Practice…Practice.

Tip 8: How to Answer Essay Questions

If your exam does not include essay questions, you may skip this chapter. Since some exams have them, here are tips on how to answer essay questions. Unlike multiple choice questions, essay questions do not have a single best suitable choice or answer. Instead, essay questions require you to demonstrate the overall quality of your thinking and writing skills.

The typical components in an Essay Question are:

1). **Prompt** – this is the setup of the essay question in essence the directions. The Prompt will ask you to either explain your point of view on an excerpt of information presented. Or, in some cases, the

Prompt will ask you to write a critique of an argument presented.

2). **Information/Subject** – this is the excerpt or reading material presented in the essay question. It is the information that you will base your writing on.

3). **Question/Assignment** – the question is in some cases called the Assignment. The question will tell you what to write about. In the question, you may have more than one stem. Sometimes the whole question may be the stem.

Steps for answering an Essay Question:

1. **Read** the **Prompt, Information/Subject, and Question/Assignment** thoroughly.

2. **Select the "Stem" or Stems of the question**. In other words, determine what the question is really asking you. The Stem is a key word or phrase that explains the theme or main purpose of the question. It gives the plot of the question.

3. **Think** about what the question is asking you to do.

4. Before you start writing**, make an outline** of your response. In the outline include:

   a. What you will include in addressing the stem(s);

   b. How you will organize your ideas;

   c. How you will develop your ideas fully or with details;

   d. What relevant supporting reasons and or examples you will use to demonstrate your point.

THE ESSAY EXAM QUESTION

Example

Prompt:

Think carefully about the issue presented in the following excerpt and assignment below:

Information/Subject:

Excerpt from President John F. Kennedy's Inaugural Address on January 20, 1961

"Now the trumpet summons us again--not as a call to bear arms, though arms we need--not as a call to battle, though embattled we are-- but a call to bear the burden of a long twilight struggle, year in and year out, "rejoicing in hope, patient in tribulation"--a struggle against the common enemies of man: tyranny, poverty, disease and war itself.

Can we forge against these enemies a grand and global alliance, North and South, East and

West, that can assure a more fruitful life for all mankind? Will you join in that historic effort?

In the long history of the world, only a few generations have been granted the role of defending freedom in its hour of maximum danger. I do not shrink from this responsibility--I welcome it. I do not believe that any of us would exchange places with any other people or any other generation. The energy, the faith, the devotion which we bring to this endeavor will light our country and all who serve it--and the glow from that fire can truly light the world.

And so, my fellow Americans: ask not what your country can do for you--ask what you can do for your country.

My fellow citizens of the world: ask not what America will do for you, but what together we can do for the freedom of man."

Assignment/Question:

How well reasoned do you find President Kennedy's arguments? Does everyone play a part in defending against the enemies of mankind? Write an essay in which you develop your point of view on this issue. Support your position with reasoning and examples taken from your reading, studies, experience or observations.

My Essay following the Steps:

1. Read the Prompt, Information/Subject, and Question/Assignment thoroughly.

I read everything – Done.

2. Select the stem(s) in the question.

The stems of the question are:

a. How well reasoned or logical are the Presidents points?

b. Does everyone play a part in defending the enemies of mankind -tyranny, poverty, disease and war? and

c. My position on the issue.

3. Think about what the question is asking you to do.

The question is asking me to express if the comments in the excerpt are well reasoned or structured; and to give my viewpoint on the question does everyone play a part in defending against the enemies of mankind? It is also asking me to give reasons and or examples to support my position.

4. Before you start writing, make an outline of your response. In the outline include:

a. What you will include in addressing the stem(s);

Answers to each question outlined in the stem(s)

b. How you will organize your ideas;

In chronological order starting with President Kennedy's viewpoint, then my viewpoint

c. How you will develop your ideas fully or with details;

Include details from the Excerpt and my experiences

d. What relevant supporting reasons and or examples you will use to demonstrate your point.

Examples from my reading and experiences

My Essay:

President Kennedy states that we have a call to bear the burden of a struggle against the common enemies of man: tyranny, poverty, disease and war. In his speech he asked both the people of America and the people of the world to join him in the fight to defend freedom. His challenge to the citizens of America was to ask not what their country could do for them but to ask what they could do for their country. To the citizens of the world he asked them to ask not what America would do for them but what together we all can do for freedom. His comments were very logical and compelling because the future of mankind is in the hands of all of mankind not just one person, group or nation.

I feel everyone does play a part in defending against the enemies of mankind because we all belong to it. Each person has a unique talent that can help in this fight against those things that keep us from being free. From the leaders of nations working together to settle world disputes and promote peace around the world through the United Nations, to people in local communities working together to feed the hungry through food banks, we all can and should play a part. Each part we play may be different and determined by our ability, resources and treasure; but we all can do something. Some of us are doctors and other medical professionals who care for the sick. While others are missionaries tending to the needs of the impoverished. Some of us are brave men and women going to war to defend the world from violence. And then, some of us may be a neighbor just sharing a ride with someone who otherwise could not go vote. The size of what each person does in the fight for freedom is not the most critical thing. Rather, the fact that we do something to assist is most important.

If all of the people of the world worked together as a **World Team for Freedom**, we can defeat our common enemies: tyranny, poverty, disease and war, because:

Together

Each person

Accomplishes

More.

Keep Calm As You Write Your Essay!

Tip 9: Make a Trial Run to the Exam Site

When your exam requires you to travel to a designated test center or site to take it, make a trial run to that location at least five days before your exam date. After you reach the test center, park, get out of your car and go to the suite or entrance of the exam site. This action is to help relieve any possible anxiety on exam day. I had a student once who did not do a trial run because she thought she knew where it was. On exam day she went to the wrong place and ended up finding the site twenty minutes after the exam started. Unfortunately, the site administrator did not allow her to take the exam that day. It took several telephone calls and pleas to the certification authorities to get her exam rescheduled without paying the fee again. It was a nerve-racking experience. Do not let that happen to you – Make a trial run to your exam site.

Sometimes the test site may be out of town and you are unable to make this trial run. If that's your situation, map out your trip using a map application such as MapQuest, Google Maps or similar application. Then, call the test site and get additional tips on how to find the location. You should complete this action at least five days before your exam.

Tip 10: Your Last Week of Study

Well, your Exam is a week away. So far on your journey, you've read your materials, taken notes, and completed practice exams. This last week is a time for review and practice exams. Go back to your notes and review all of the important information you recorded. Next, practice the Test-taking Techniques by retaking all of your practice exams. I know this sounds repetitive; but it's critical to memorizing the Test-taking Techniques.

When you retake your practice exams, review questions you missed the first time you took the exam(s). From the missed questions, listen to your recorded reading about that subject. If you did not record yourself, then go back to the materials and reread the section(s) covering that topic to gain a better understanding. Retake all practice exams at least twice or until you get a passing score of 90% or higher on each.

Remember, the major key to passing your Exam is to become skilled at applying the Test-taking Techniques to answer questions. You gain this skill by practicing. The more you practice taking exams the better you become at taking them. In your last week of study, devote 90% of your study time to completing practice exams. Retake your exams over and over and over, it will be tiring; but I promise you it will be worth it on Exam Day.

Tip 11: The Day Before Your Exam

Well you are almost to your destination, Exam Day.

On the day before your Big Day, please:

1. Stop studying by 12 o'clock noon. You've read the materials; prepared and reviewed your notes; practiced the test-taking techniques. You are Ready. To avoid over studying and possibly creating undue stress for yourself, you need to stop at noon.

2. Review your registration and admissions information. Assemble all required documents you need for tomorrow. Put this information in your wallet, purse or car so you will not forget anything tomorrow morning.

3. Layout the clothes you will wear. If your Vision included a certain outfit, make sure you prepare it for tomorrow. Since many test centers are often cold inside, include a light sweater or jacket with your clothes. Be sure to wear comfortable clothing that complies with the test center's dress code, if applicable.

4. Eat a healthy, wholesome dinner.

5. Rest your mind and body by going to bed early and getting a good night's sleep.

Remember to read your "WHY" and visualize

"Passing the Exam" before you go to sleep.

IT'S EXAM DAY!

Tip 12: Exam Day

Today is the end of your journey. It's Exam Day - Your Destination. You are probably excited and nervous at the same time. Before you start your day, review your "Why" and "Vision" of passing the exam. Visualize the words, "Congratulations You Passed."

Here are my final tips before you go claim your Reward:

1. Eat eggs for breakfast. Eggs are the **best brain** food and helps with what I call waking up the brain and improving your memory. Eggs especially their yolks contain high concentrations of Choline an essential nutrient that is important for memory. In addition, eggs are a good source of iron, a mineral

needed to produce oxygen-carrying hemoglobin in the blood. According to the American Heart Association, eggs can be part of a heart-healthy diet as long as you consume no more than 300 milligrams of cholesterol a day and one egg has only 185 milligrams. All you need to eat is one egg – prepared any way you wish.

2. Limit your intake of coffee and other liquids so you are not running to the restroom a lot during the exam.

3. Get to the exam site early.

4. Breathe – take deep breaths to calm yourself down. You can also calm yourself down by

thinking of something that makes your laugh. So calm down and Laugh.

5. Observe all of the instructions from the site administrator. Pay close attention to what that person tells you. The site administrator has answers to any questions you may have, so Listen and Comply.

6. Start the Exam:

- Read the instructions completely;
- Use the test-taking techniques when answering the questions;
- Skip any question that you do not know the answer to, mark it, and go back to it before you submit the exam for grading. When you

go back to the question, use the test-taking techniques to select the answer that appears the most logical or reasonable;

- Answer all of the questions;

- Think positively and refrain from changing your answers;

- Go back through the exam once more to ensure you answered all questions;

- Close your eyes and visualize one more time the words "Congratulations, You Passed;"

- Claim your Reward;

- Click the bottom – Submit your Exam Answers.

WOW, you did it. It's time to Celebrate.

Let me be the first one to say…

CONGRATULATIONS, YOU PASSED!

You Made It!

Your Journey Is Over!

Testimonies: Hear What Others Say

"Betty has extraordinary insight and a caring spirit. She has been my personal mentor for many years. She truly cares about people and wants to help them succeed. In this book, she shares techniques and tips that I have witnessed are proven to work. Many of my direct reports have attended Betty's study groups and have had 100% pass rate on their exams! What I like about Betty's techniques are that she provides a simple, common sense plan, breaking it down and providing a formula to follow. Having a plan lends to a better success rate and creates a more comfortable, stress-free test day."

Denise Fowler, CPP, PHR | Manager- Client Learning Services | MAS Learning & Performance

###

'The seeds of my career in curriculum design and test development were planted, nourished, and nurtured in the time I worked for and with Betty Moore. Specifically, her cogent and pinpoint direction on test-taking strategies enabled me, very early in my career, to get to the heart of the problem and, by design, respond correctly, effectively, and confidently. Get to the stem, and you can get to the roots. That philosophy can do more than just answer test questions."

Whitney L. Jones, CPP, PHR |
Instructional Designer | Learning & Performance
ADP, LLC | Major Account Services | Business
Engineering Solutions

###

"I've had the honor of friendship with Betty McKenzie Moore for 14 years and counting. And I have to say that "Congratulations, You Passed! Test-taking Techniques & Tips for Passing Exams," is a phenomenal book. It is an easy read with great simplicity. It also equips you with the fundamental tools for taking exams such as but not limited to the Sat and the Act, Professional license exams as well as Certification exams. Implementing this book to your personal library aids you not only in passing the exam it also gives you the confidence and focus needed, being one myself to have experienced nervousness and anxiety when taking exams such as the Board of Realtors or the State Board of Cosmetology as well as Certification of makeup artistry, allows me to understand the great impact that "Congratulations, You Passed! Test-taking Techniques & Tips for Passing Exams" will have on exam-takers across the board!"

Sabrina Watkins – Entrepreneur & Business Owner

###

"As we travel through life many of us are challenged in particular areas... Taking & passing a critical test is one of them. A teacher here, a mentor there, contributes to our "Dictionary" of Testing knowledge. Betty has taken the most important aspects involved in passing an exam &

articulated them into a foolproof plan for advancing oneself in the twenty-first century. Every student & professional will find something in this book that will help him to achieve his goals. What a privilege it is to have been among those, who have seen it first!"

Elaine OBrzut Coyle – Retired Teacher & Business Owner

###

"I decided to take the SPHR exam in May 2002. Many of my colleagues at ADP also would be taking the certification exam at this time. Our peer Betty Moore ran a prep course which we had heard was helpful on many levels so I signed up. As it turns out this course was incredibly helpful in my passing this difficult and rigorous exam. It taught me the following:

1. How to eliminate 2 out of the 4 WRONG answers. With half the options gone, your

likelihood of selecting the right answer is greater

2. How to really understand what the question means. By doing a quick analysis of what the heart of the question is helps to select the right answer

3. Time management

4. Often your gut is right on when you are truly torn between a few answers that both feel correct

5. Testing often was helpful

6. How to relax and not feel overwhelmed during the test which only inhibits your ability to select correct answers

7. Working in a group setting is very helpful for comparing test taking techniques

8. Regular meetings ensure that I was able to continue my readings and not "fall behind"

Betty's enthusiasm and positivity created a coach like mentality with the team and was inspirational. VAST majority of the people in my group passed and this course was a HUGE reason why."

Doug Hilton - Head of HR Operations - East Hub at Ericsson

About the Author

Betty McKenzie Moore is the Founder of The Employment Front, LLC a business specializing in Human Resources (HR) and Management Consulting that provides businesses with workplace solutions through training, consulting and coaching services. As a retired ADP human resource executive, Ms. Moore has over 32 years of experience in HR management & training, payroll, civil rights and employment law compliance. While at ADP, Ms. Moore's scope of responsibility included the Central and Southeastern United States and Puerto Rico. She also served as an Adjunct Professor at ADP University.

For the past 15 years, Ms. Moore conducted HR certification preparatory classes for the Society for Human Resource Management (SHRM®) Professional in Human Resources (PHR) and Senior Professional in Human Resources (SPHR) certification exams. Using the same techniques and tips in her book, *Congratulations, You Passed! Test-taking Techniques & Tips for Passing Exams*, she helped over 900 students pass the HR certification exams on their first try.

From a personal standpoint over the span of 20+ years, Ms. Moore honed her techniques and tips on herself by using them when she took and passed the following exams on her first try:

1. Senior Professional in Human Resources (SPHR) certification exam
2. Certified Professional Coach (CPC) certification exam
3. Certified Payroll Professional (CPP) certification exam
4. DDI Certified Facilitator - Development Dimensions International's certification exam
5. MBTI® Certified – Myers-Briggs Type Indicator® certification exam
6. State of Georgia Licensed Real Estate Salesperson exam
7. State of Georgia Licensed Real Estate Broker exam.

Betty McKenzie Moore holds a B.S. Degree in Education from Louisiana State University (LSU) and is a frequent speaker for organizations throughout the Southeast.

She lives in Fayetteville, GA with her husband, Calvin.

###

THANK YOU!

Made in the USA
Middletown, DE
23 February 2020